TELL ME WHERE YOU'RE STUCK

A Handbook for
Moving Forward into More Success

Helen Racz

TELL ME WHERE YOU'RE STUCK

A Handbook for
Moving Forward into More Success

Leneh Publishing
Houston, Texas

By Helen Racz
All Rights Reserved © 2019 by Helen Racz

Published by Leneh Publishing
Printed in the United States of America

Author: Helen Racz
Book Cover Design: AlphaGraphics of West Houston
Book Design: Caroline Carruba, AlphaGraphics of West Houston

13-digit ISBN: 978-1-7331896-0-6
Library of Congress Control Number: 2019911048

1. Business- Psychology 2. Sales-Success
First Edition: August 2019

Leneh Publishing is available for printing at special quantity discounts for use as premiums and sales promotions, or for use in corporate trainings or as conference materials. For more information, please contact Sales at LenehBookSales@gmail.com.

For Rosa Glenn Reilly

Thank you for being the living example of

paying it forward generously for

the joy of the ripple effect of

spreading good.

I appreciate all your mentoring and

support over all these years

CONTENTS

"No one saves us
but ourselves
No one can
and no one may.
We ourselves
must walk the path."

–Buddha

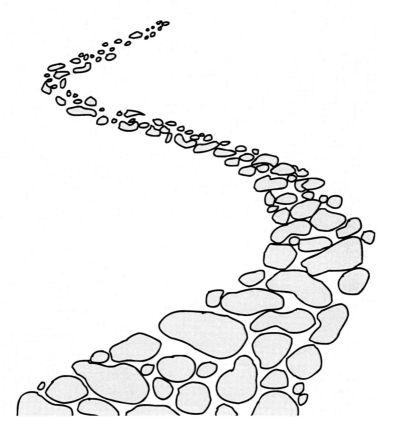

A WORD FROM HELEN

Hello Reader, and thank you for picking up this book. I'm happy to share this information with you because I am certain you can benefit from it.

For years I knew I wanted to write a book in honor of all the teachers that came into my life through books. I thought of it as checking off the "pay it forward" item on my bucket list. After teaching life coaching classes for over a decade, with many requests from students for the book version to reference and share, I was put in touch with a ghost writer. I had seen my students and clients find success by applying my teachings, and I finally felt that I had something worthy of sharing. So, I was ready to write a book, but just didn't know how to organize the material and needed a writer's perspective. So, Dr. Cindy Childress watched some of my teaching videos, interviewed me for 20 plus hours and began writing the *Logical Law of Attraction* ("LLOA"). What an undertaking it was to put spiritual teachings together cohesively! Cindy had to quickly evolve her consciousness, as did I, into even more clarity. We ended up co-authoring the book because she shares her experience of learning the information while ghost-writing that book.

During the LLOA book writing process, I was blessed to meet Karen McCullough who encouraged me to write a book for the corporate sector, which I had not previously considered. Realizing I often coach many clients who are not into spiritual teachings, I agreed because both Karen and I see people of all lifestyles and belief systems who are seeking a better life experience. When I mentioned to Karen that I love coaching, she asked how I start with clients, and I replied that I often begin with, "Tell me where you're stuck."

Karen thought it the right title and directed me to get it written and get back with her. In the process of writing this book, I led a retreat and whipped out a workbook format. At the time, I was scheduled to be a presenter in a conference where I would also teach this information, which gave me a hard deadline to get this book published so that I could take both the book and the workbook format along with me. Being in the process of writing two books at the same time has stretched me in all the ways I most enjoy. In addition, it aligned me to my intention that every reader will also respond to the invitation to stretch into ever-expanding success.

ACKNOWLEDGMENTS

The truth is I could never actually thank all the many people who are a part of the concepts that I am sharing in this book, because each and every author, student, client, friend and family member who is a part of my life is also part of my growth into the understanding shared in this book. I feel blessed to have so many incredible people in my life in so many diverse ways. And I sincerely feel gratitude for everyone willing to learn how to have the best experience possible in life.

Input from countless authors stretched my consciousness through ideas and facts and possibilities. I thank them all for everything they have given to me although they don't even know me or how much they have impacted my life. Fascinating!

Thank you to my husband, Greg, for loving and supporting me through all my many life chapters. We've been married since 1989. Sometimes I wonder whether he feels like he's been married to many different women—the one with chronic pain, the mother of his children, the one who loves and adores him, the child care provider, the real estate investor, the gym owner, the spiritual seeker, the artist, the teacher and now the author. He sees me in all my identities and simply flows with the changes as I expand. I always think he's amazing, and I love his stability that allows me so much room to explore.

I thank my sons for being incredible adults (in my mind they make me look good) and for being part of my learning and living successfully as a person and as a parent. I especially appreciate all the questions and reminders of how to think that we truly learned at the same time!

I also thank my students, without whom my life wouldn't be so much fun! Through teaching them what I thought I knew, I taught myself even more. Being able to witness so many people's successful results kept me infused with enthusiasm.

I am grateful for all of my clients. As I coached, I learned how to speak to different people in different ways the one pivotal truth: we can be successful in anything we choose. I also humbly thank them for the trust they placed in me to guide them in helping themselves.

I thank Stephen Covey for the one book to which I give most credit for my success in all my relationships, *The 7 Habits of Highly Effective People*. He introduced me to the principles I use consistently, and although it was many years before I realized how it all fit logically, his book is truly the greatest gift I ever gave myself! It took me years of reading it daily to learn how to practice it consistently. After all, I had never met anyone who consistently lived any one of the principles taught in Covey's book. And, it was worth every struggle.

A great big thank you to Sue Murchison for connecting me to Karen McCullough and for leading me into the adventure of getting this book created and published.

To Karen McCullough, I say a special word of thanks, not only for the title of this book, but also for encouraging me to bring my teaching to the business world.

I send a special thank you to the first readers for their time and feedback, Nancy Kidd, Sharon Sawallisch, Laura Williams, Alana Allingham, Alan Anderson and Shelby Hamilton.

Racine Byers, thank you so much for initial line editing and giving me the bonus of which sentences spoke the most to you. Positive feedback is so supportive!

Thanks also to Dulcie Wink for countless hours of developmental editing, brainstorming with me over word choice and helping organize this teaching into the outline it has become. It was a generous and expansive experience, blessing both me and my readers.

Thanks to Jessica Woods of Infiniti Graphics, Houston, Texas.

Thank you, Amber Hibbard and Caroline Carruba of AlphaGraphics of West Houston, for holding my hand in the last (and yet so visual) stages of bringing this book into fruition—the cover, book layout and printing.

I also thank Paige Manginello for the photo of me for back cover.

"Happiness is when what you think, what you say and what you do are in harmony."

–*Mahatma Gandhi*

CHAPTER I
How We Got Here

When people come to me for help, I ask them, "Tell me what you want?" Or, if they've already told me what they want, I say, "Tell me where you're stuck." Both questions are designed to figure out where they're stuck. If a person doesn't have what she wants, or is in a repeating cycle that doesn't produce the results she wants, then she's stuck. She isn't getting the success she wants.

As I listen to the clients' answers, I can identify where they are missing (or misapplying) essential elements for success. I am writing this book to give people a formula and instructional handbook that can help them get out of the pain of being stuck.

How did I get here? It's interesting that I wound up coaching people to find success in their lives, because I used to envy people who knew what they wanted to do when they grew up—people who went to college and then followed a direct path to success.

Before I discovered what I wanted to do for my career, a car accident in 1987 changed my life in incredible ways. Unbelievably challenging, it left me with herniated disks and chronic pain, which led me to drop out of art school (my hands would go numb) and also drop out of college because the neck pain made it difficult to study, test, and keep up with life as a working mother and wife. An unexpected blessing, that accident led me into many entrepreneurial ventures and into energy work for relief from pain. The energy work led me into a fascinating study of vibration that continues to intrigue me. The vibrational perspective crosses easily into all belief systems without offending religious, scientific or medical perspectives.

I literally grew my understanding of the information I'm sharing here through teaching about vibrational law. And, what a fabulous difference it has made in all areas of my life and in the lives of countless clients and students! I intend that you, too, will find positive results in your own application.

I often say with confidence and ease: "I have no idea what life will be like next . . . what might happen. I do, however, know how I'll show up!" This is true because I know how to think. In its essence, this book is a handbook about how (not what) to think so that you can consistently find your way to success, even when you hit a challenge and feel stuck.

People often get stuck in a repeating cycle that prevents them from achieving what they want. By learning the formula (essential elements) for success and following the handbook that I present in this book, people can guide themselves out of the sticky cycles and back into success. Being aware of the elements and the dynamics helps build confidence in the ability to take clear, consistent action that is designed to achieve what we want.

In this book, we will explore how and why people get stuck. I will present a formula and handbook for getting out of that frustrating situation, whatever it may be.

Because the formula and handbook involve changing the way we think, we need to first discuss obstacles to learning a new way of thinking. The handbook only works when we follow the rules of engagement. Once the obstacles, formula and rules of engagement are understood, we will explore how four simple handbook questions, *when applied under the rules of engagement*, can propel you to the success you seek.

CHAPTER II
Being Stuck

It can feel like you're doing everything right. You're a good person, you mean well, you show up and try to do the right thing. Yet, there seems to be disappointment more often than ease. Frustration seems normal or at least usual, with no clear explanation of why or how to regularly experience more successful outcomes.

Why do we get stuck? I believe that we are here in this experience that we call life to consistently evolve and expand. If you look all around you at nature, history, science, medicine and even religion, it's all about expansion and change. The feeling of being stuck signals us that it's time to expand our perspective, evolve our understanding. It indicates we have outgrown a belief system or an expectation that is holding us back from our natural instinctual desire to evolve into something more and better than we are in the present moment. Unless hindered by injury or illness, everything on earth wants to grow and evolve.

Humans do not experience fulfillment without experiencing challenge. Without overcoming challenge, we end up in ruts and stuck in a way that leads to boredom, unhappiness and sometimes ends in depression.

How does the need for challenge and fulfillment apply in business?

Find a company with both long-term financial success and a happy workforce, and you'll likely learn that it is run by people who understand the importance of setting the stage for employees to thrive. The company consistently uses principles that benefit the business, its employees, its customers and others in the community. The opposite is a company with a lot of turnover, or with employees who don't enjoy their work and only keep showing up for their paychecks. Sadly, this is more often the norm, and its internal stagnation causes so much stress and sickness in our culture. The same can be said for any organizations or groups, including families. Without applying principles for thinking (and acting) that are designed to bring about expansion for more good, then we can become stuck in a looping or repeating cycle that causes frustration or emotional struggle. Sound familiar?

When people feel stuck, they feel they are not succeeding. For example:

- An adult might repeatedly become emotionally triggered when dealing with his parent;

- A person in a romantic relationship could be having repeated conflict with her spouse about money, parenting, vacation planning, etc.;

- A person could be stuck in a job or career he doesn't like, but not know what kind of job or career to pursue next;

- A business can become stuck when it is not meeting its goals for growth, new product lines, etc.

Success to me is unlimited creativity. For purposes of this book, I define "creativity" as making something that didn't exist before. Knowing how to think (applying this handbook) allows me to avoid getting stuck and achieve creativity that flows as fast as my life changes, which in turn challenges me to create new ways to contribute, explore and be. Think how often life changes: kids grow, interests and styles change, economies vary, work demands cycle, bodies age, technology advances.... I want to be creative throughout every change life throws at me.

Regardless of how you personally define success, this book is about identifying where and why you have become stuck on the road to that success, as well as the way to get unstuck.

Stuck. It is being in a repeating pattern and not knowing how to think or act in a way that leads to positive change.

Getting unstuck. It involves using clarity in thought to take right action. It involves applying a formula for success. And, there are rules of engagement when applying the formula!

The following quote is often attributed to Einstein, although there is significant debate as to whether he actually said it:

"Insanity is doing the same thing over and over again and expecting different results."

If we, as human beings, want to have the change that we prefer, it begins with taking personal responsibility for changing our way of thinking. Everything begins with thought. If a person doesn't have the results they're seeking, they haven't applied the right formula for their own thinking.

Perhaps Thomas Edison said it best:

"Five percent of the people think; ten percent of the people think they think; and the other eighty-five percent would rather die than think."

–Thomas A. Edison

If you're reading this book you are NOT in the 85% who don't want to think or question their thought processes. Yet, that other 85% is a large percentage, which may explain why so many individuals (and sometimes society as a whole) are stuck in repeating patterns.

You, on the other hand, think. And, because you're reading this book, you are willing to change your way of thinking, or at least to consider doing so if it will help you get unstuck in one or more areas of your life.

"THE MIND IS
EVERYTHING.
WHAT YOU THINK,
YOU BECOME."

–Gautama Buddha

CHAPTER III
It's All About Thought

Everything humans create begins with thought. So, it should come as no surprise that getting unstuck requires thought.

"Self-discipline begins with the mastery of your thoughts. If you don't control what you think, you can't control what you do. Simply, self-discipline enables you to think first and act afterward."

–Napoleon Hill, Think and Grow Rich

We are long past the era when "necessity is the mother of invention." Today, we can create things for the sheer joy of the experience. We have hair dyes in every conceivable hue, electronic pianos, wearable art, 3-D movies, telephones with cameras, heated and cooled automobile seats, none of which are necessities.

Our minds can conceive limitless inventions, but each creation begins with a single thought (an idea or concept), followed by many more thoughts necessary to design and build it. For example, many thoughts were needed to imagine, design and build the chair in which you are sitting. Someone had to conceive the size, weight, materials, style, design and functionality. More thoughts and decisions were necessary to manufacture, market, sell and deliver the chair to the customer so that you could sit in it today.

Jumbled thoughts are less effective in the process of creating something useful. Clarity in thought is critical.

Have you ever wondered what thought is? Have you considered whether and to what extent thought affects what we achieve or experience? Beliefs influence our thoughts. Our beliefs and the words we speak can shape our lives and drive us toward success and happiness or failure and distress.

Our thoughts and actions can profoundly affect our ability to create the change we want in our lives. We have all seen this in action. A happy person tends to attract more happiness to himself, whereas an angry person finds much about which to be angry. The peaceful person tends to live a peaceful life, while a melodramatic person endlessly finds people and circumstances with which to create more drama. These are examples of the principle: Like attracts like.

Healthy, slim people tend to think and feel differently about food and movement than people who are prone to weight and health issues. Comedians think differently than most of us; they observe everyday life and then present it in a way that allows the rest of us to see the humor in the mundane. A millionaire thinks and feels about money differently than a billionaire. An entrepreneur thinks and feels differently about work and investing than an employee.

I raise these axioms here to suggest that you consider what kinds of thoughts will help you travel faster on your road to the success you want to create. Aligning your thoughts to those who have (or who have achieved) whatever success you want can expedite your path to gaining it.

If you seek happiness, for example, it is important to begin thinking, seeing, speaking and believing of things the way a happy person does. If you seek financial ease, it is important to begin thinking as a financially successful person does. If you want a more peaceful relationship with someone, it is important to be a highly peaceful person in the relationship.

The phrase "wherever you go, there you are" is a summary of a story in *Alcoholics Anonymous: The Story of How Many Thousands of Men and Women Have Recovered from Alcoholism*—a book written by William G. ("Bill W.") Wilson, first published in 1939 and generally known as "The Big Book" due to the thickness of the paper used in the first edition. The phrase means that moving away from a problem—geographically or otherwise—will not solve it; instead, we carry it with us until we resolve it

Wherever you go, you take your dominant thought patterns with you. Thus, if you are thinking that great things only happen to "other people," you may be placing roadblocks in your path to success. Positive thoughts, words and actions align you to positive change. Negative thought can lead you to become stuck in repeating negative patterns.

You witness people with positive dominant thought patterns all around you. You see evidence of what their positive thought patterns create. The trick is finding your own patterns and transforming them into a match for what you prefer in life.

CHAPTER IV
Obstacles to Changing Our Way of Thinking

Changing our way of thinking can be challenging because we tend to want to avoid change, and because our minds are wired to filter out many existing types of physical, mental, instinctual and vibrational information. In addition, a part of the human mind also hates to be wrong, and for many, learning new things seems to cause distress.

1. Humans tend to resist learning new things

Change is inevitable. Everyone's capacity to enjoy life is linked to their ease (comfort with) adapting to change, which requires continuous learning. Top surgeons must learn new cutting-edge technology that is developed for surgical procedures. Marketing professionals who worked in the "old days" of only print, radio and television advertising had to learn to apply their trade to social media platforms like Facebook, Twitter and others. When CAD (computer aided design) was created, draftsmen who were taught only manual drafting had to learn CAD to be competitive.

Change is also inevitable outside of the world of technology. Singers learn better ways to develop and protect their vocal cords. Athletes benefit from new training methods. New parents benefit from parenting classes and advances in child psychology.

Most highly successful leaders choose to continue to learn, whether through reading, attending seminars or meeting with people about new methods and processes. Bill Gates is known for retreating to a cottage once or more per year for a "Think Week" in which he spends his time reading and thinking about the future of technology and how he will lead Microsoft into that future.

"Progress is impossible without change, and those who cannot change their minds cannot change anything."
–*George Bernard Shaw*

Although children expect to keep learning new things, many adults choose to stop learning. Adults sometimes feel threatened or uncomfortable when someone points out a new or different way of experiencing life. If a person didn't have good learning experiences in school, he may not want to learn something new. If a person had a bad experience learning to use e-mail, she may be even less interested in using a social media platform to keep up with friends and relatives.

Learning involves trying something new and sometimes struggling to get it right. We resist the part of learning that involves making mistakes until we master a new way of doing something—thinking, in this case.

Our mind doesn't want to be wrong; it is threatened by the possibility of being proven wrong. Why? It may arise, in part, from the deeply instinctive human need for survival. In ancient human history, being wrong—more specifically, acting against a tribe's rules—could result in being thrown out of the tribe. Survival without the tribe's support could be difficult or impossible. *Fatal.*

Even today, we learn from an early age that being wrong can sometimes be fatal. We teach our children not to cross the street without first looking both ways; otherwise, the child could be injured or killed by a car.

Once the instinct to avoid being wrong kicks in, people tend to blame others instead of taking responsibility for their own actions. Examples include the adulterer blaming the spouse, the abuser blaming the abused, and the rapist blaming the victim.

All of these examples illustrate that it is important for us to realize that we may tend to resist learning something new.

2. Our minds filter out information

The mind, itself, presents another challenge to learning a new way of thinking because it is always *filtering* out information. The mind performs physical filtering, relational filtering and vibrational (or instinctive) filtering.

a. Physical Filtering
Consider that, in any given moment, all of our senses are constantly bombarded by signals, such as: the sounds of people talking, music playing and traffic noise; the sight of flashing lights; etc. Without one level of mind filtering information, we would have great difficulty functioning. In fact, some people have trouble filtering and, as a result, experience great difficulty focusing amidst the typical sights and sounds that are naturally filtered out by most people's minds. When we go to a movie, for example, most of us tune out the sights and sounds of other people shifting in their seats, eating popcorn, and whispering, as well as the hum of the air conditioning. Without that filtering, the movie would not be an enjoyable experience. (Crying babies are hard to tune out.)

In every moment, all of our senses are constantly receiving millions of bits of information. Imagine how much more you can hear if you stop and totally focus only on hearing. You can do the same with your senses of sight, smell, taste and touch. You can sense the temperature of the room, the texture of clothing, the feel of your shoes, jewelry and hair, as well as the feel of whatever you sit on (hard, soft, comfortable or not). You can sense your body at work— digestion, pain, health, etc. Your taste buds also constantly read input, including the toxins you exhale if you haven't recently drunk or eaten anything.

Each sensory system is constantly processing an enormous amount of data. All of it would cause total overload if your brain didn't filter out some, or most, of the physical data so you can focus.

b. Relational Filtering
Another aspect in which the mind filters out information is by absorbing only what it finds relatable or interesting. If I heard a lecture on higher math, science or medicine, it wouldn't take long for me to begin daydreaming because I couldn't link the subject matter to anything I already knew. My mind would pay attention to only a very small portion of the lecture. I might tune back into speaker's humor or mannerisms, to words that I knew, or to things that I'd find of interest, as opposed to information that didn't make sense to my existing thought framework. This is why you can ask a group of people about a lecture they attended and get varying viewpoints, from their individual perceptions.

c. Vibrational or Instinctual Filtering
It also helps to understand the bigger picture of how we interact at a vibrational level in order to see why we often feel stuck. It helps to understand why it is challenging to move forward once we're stuck in a frustrating existing pattern.

Science today teaches us that everything is energy. Everything is in motion—you, me, everything. Even things that appear solid are truly made of atoms vibrating at a certain frequency. As a result, everything on this plane of existence is about vibration. If you hear a cricket you'll soon hear another join in. Put two grandfather clocks against the same wall and eventually their pendulums will sync up. Similarly, when a group of women live together in a dorm, their menstrual cycles tend to end up on the same schedule. If you have two pianos in a hall and play one note by pressing a key on one piano, the matching string on the other piano will also vibrate.

When a group of people are amidst the energy of an angry mob (mob energy), people who succumb to the energy will do things they would normally never do on their own. To the contrary, a charismatic speaker can lift and elevate the spirit of thousands of people through the cohesive field that he emanates as he speaks.

People believe we receive most information from the words we hear and things we see. Yet, we actually also sense important information in the form of energy through what I call the energetic body, or the auric field. This is why you can "feel" when someone is staring at you. You don't sense a *physical* touch when someone is merely looking in your direction, but your energetic field definitely receives the energy resonance of the other person's focus.

We can sense, respond and react to another person's energy. In a crisis, people sometimes automatically look to a person who is a natural leader, despite not knowing her previously. They sense her leadership qualities.

Unfortunately, most of us are taught to override our trust in this type of sensory input at a very young age. We are taught to be polite to everyone regardless of how we feel about them. A friend of mine, for example, explained that her very sensitive daughter didn't like a man who she encountered at her school. Yet, the girl was often "corrected" by being told to be polite to him. Later, it was learned that the man was a child molester. My friend's daughter had a gut-instinctive *feeling* that there was something dangerous or untrustworthy about the man. Conversely, children in our society are also often taught to fear all strangers, when in reality they may one day need a *trustworthy* stranger's assistance when lost or in other danger. Parents cannot teach their children to develop good gut instincts unless the parents have personally developed their own instincts.

In the movie the *Girl with The Dragon Tattoo*, there is an excellent example of this. The murderer invites in the reporter. Once he has the reporter bound and gagged, the murderer points out that the reporter didn't want to come in, but did so to be polite, just as every other victim did. We are taught to only use information that fits the social norm.

Great investors often have a sixth sense, or gut knowing, about timing—when to buy, sell or hold. It may arise, in part, from their ability to perceive the movement of the markets or market trends at a vibrational level that most of us envy. If you can think of our reality as vibrational, you can take it out of the personal realm and see from a perspective that helps you without making you wrong.

"If you want to find the secrets of the universe, think in terms of energy, frequency and vibration."

–Nikola Tesla

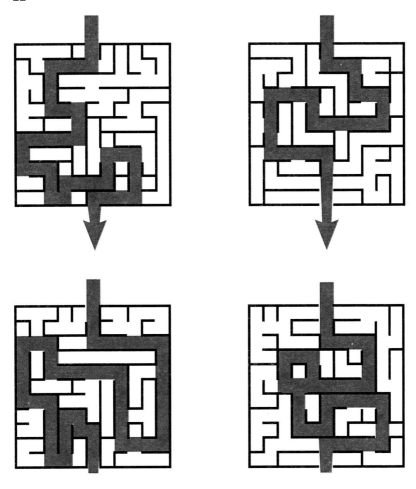

3. Existing patterns and habits get in our way

Patterns of many kinds also exist and persist as another obstacle to changing the way we think because we tend to act consistently (habitually) with existing thought patterns. You can see them everywhere in the form of historical patterns, experiential patterns and physical patterns.

a. Historical Patterns

Historical patterns of thinking tend to be repeated and are generally slow to change. Throughout history, prejudicial thought patterns have existed, whether based on race, gender, culture, religion or sexual orientation. The longer a pattern has existed, the longer people have seen, absorbed, accepted (often without question) and taken action in line with the pattern. Thus, the effort and energy required to change a thought pattern increases in relation to the length of time the pattern has existed.

The movies *Hidden Figures* and *The Green Book* are excellent examples of how much effort, time and energy it took to evolve old prejudicial thought patterns. People had to consistently show up in the old energy and thought pattern (being treated disrespectfully and unfairly) and act differently than predicted by prejudicial thinkers (with dignity and competence) for many years until things began to change.

b. Experiential Patterns

Patterns of thought, and the behavior that follows, are sometimes created as a result of human experience. Our life experiences create a paradigm—a perceptional filter or overlay—through which we view everything. For example, when siblings are asked to describe their childhood, each will describe his or her childhood differently, especially as to their individual childhood relationships with their parents. They had different perceptions because each actually had different experiences.

c. Physical Patterns

We are all familiar with patterns that arise from the way our minds work with our physical bodies. When well-practiced, we call them habits.

When we attempt to brush our teeth with our non-dominant hand, our mind and body rebels. Our dominant hand is well-programmed and practiced in our everyday tasks; the other is not. The dominant hand has established a polished habit for brushing the teeth.

When first learning, the art of driving feels overwhelmingly complex. It takes countless hours of practice before a new driver becomes comfortable with all of the driving skills. Once the skills are mastered, the driver will become relaxed enough to drive while carrying on a conversation with a passenger. Suddenly, his conscious attention may be primarily on the conversation, rather than driving. He may then drive many miles without being conscious of how he got from place to place. The conscious mind no longer has to pay attention to the complexity of driving safely.

It is a blessing when the driver can multitask driving and conversation. It is also the point where obstacles can arise. Every car is unique. Thus, when the driver gets a new car or a rental, he will need to become conscious of how it performs differently from the car he has been routinely driving. Similarly, once accustomed to driving one route to commute to and from work, a change of office requires us to pay attention to where we're going.

When a pattern has been repeated so many times that it becomes habit, it becomes unconscious. Effectively, we operate on autopilot. This occurs with all types of patterns, whether historical, experiential or physical. Thus, they can become obstacles to learning how to think differently.

Until overcome, all obstacles can limit our ability to expand successfully, whether as individuals, families, businesses, organizations or society as a whole.

CHAPTER V
The Formula (or Essential Elements) for Success

After years of working as a life coach with individuals and groups, I have recognized that every person is experienced in creating success (however one defines it) in countless ways. When stuck, however, a person hasn't identified where she is missing an ingredient to the formula for success.

Yes, there is a formula! In this context, I use the term "formula" to mean a set of four essential elements (ingredients), rather than a list of instructions.

You unconsciously use the formula all the time in every way in which you are being successful. Yet, when you're stuck in a repeating pattern and are not getting the results you want, it is because you haven't yet identified what parts of the formula for success are missing. It is not because you're slow, or wrong; it is because you can't see the forest for the trees. No one has shown you the method for thinking that will get you to success.

In this chapter, I introduce the four essential elements for any success, however you choose to define it. After all, success is a personal matter; everyone defines it differently. Your success is what is important to you.

This book then provides four questions (in Chapter VII) which, **when used under the rules of engagement** (explained in Chapter VI), will help you ensure that you are using all four of the essential elements for creating success. When we are stuck, the four questions must be asked and answered to help drive us to the missing element(s).

Is the process easy? Yes, once you have *practiced your way into mastery.*

The essential elements

Everything that humans create is established the same way, through clear and consistent thought, belief and actions. Every. Single. Thing.

Thus, the formula for creating any success is comprised of four essential elements:

- **Clarity;**

- **Belief;**

- **Action; and**

- **Consistency.**

Let's explore the logic of why each of these elements is essential for success, whether you want to create a product, change an aspect of a relationship or pursue a new career.

Let's first consider inventors and companies known for creating new and innovative products: Thomas Edison (light bulb), the Wright Brothers (airplane), Henry Ford (automobile), Ransom E. Olds (assembly line), Dr. Martin Cooper (cell phone), Bill Gates (Microsoft Inc. licensed the MS-DOS operating system for IBM's first personal computer), Steve Jobs (Apple Inc. created the iPod).

All of these "firsts" and innovators changed our world in countless ways. The innovators all had clarity about what they wanted to create. They believed that their inventions would ultimately work, although there was not yet anything on the market like their products. They acted on their beliefs by working countless hours, constantly refining their inventions through trial and error. They were consistent in their beliefs and actions, despite the setbacks that occurred when initial designs didn't fully work as anticipated. Once their inventions were proven, then many others thought of new possibilities and created new and improved designs. There are many different types of light bulbs and airplanes today, for example. But, none of the original products (or their improvements) would have been created without all four elements—clarity, belief, action and consistency.

Note that the elements overlap. Clarity is required throughout the process—first on the imagined end product, and then on refinements to the product that are discovered to be necessary through the "trial and error" phase of building and testing the prototype products. Beliefs were also refined in that process as the inventors learned what did and didn't work in their designs. Consistency is required throughout the process of gaining clarity, holding and growing beliefs, and taking actions to create the invention.

As I will illustrate through some examples in Chapter IX, the same formula also applies when a person wants to change a repeating cycle to become more successful in a relationship or in a new career path. One must have clarity, belief, action and be consistent.

There are other ways to break down elements of success. In 1989, Stephen Covey's book, *The 7 Habits of Highly Effective People*, was published. I read it in 1998 and kept reading it daily for over two years. Covey had learned that highly successful individuals, companies and organizations practice one or more of the seven habits. Yet, I had never met a single person who practiced any of them (much less all seven) consistently.

In the foreword to his book, Covey explains that he doesn't take credit for the 7 spiritual principles, which he coined as "habits," because they have always existed. I realized that *using all seven habits together* will always create the best possible outcome. One day, as I was following through with a student's request and breaking down Covey's seven habits from a spiritual perspective, I began to realize that the seven habits are actually a manual about how to *think*. I then began focusing on teaching principle-based thought.

I often recommend Covey's book to my students and clients because I often notice that people are failing to apply (or are misapplying) the principles. Sometimes, I notice that people who studied the habits will implement some or all of the principles in their work lives, but not in their personal lives.

For many, simply understanding and applying the four questions and the formula in this book is enough for a very successful life. Others will find it fascinating and empowering to go even deeper into principle-based thought and vibrational law. It all depends on what you want. This book is for those desiring more consistency in success in the mainstream. For those who want the spiritual aspects of conscious co-creation, *The Logical Law of Attraction* is my book written from that perspective.

"KNOWING IS NOT ENOUGH;
WE MUST APPLY.
WILLING IS NOT ENOUGH;
WE MUST DO."

*–Johann Wolfgang
von Goethe*

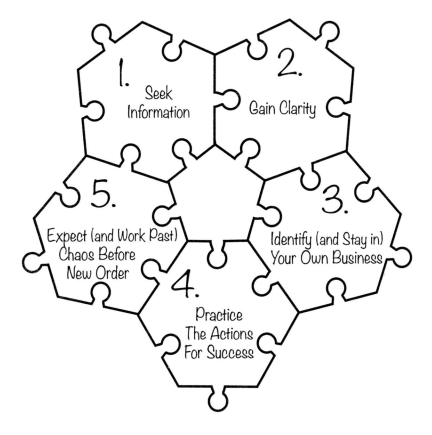

CHAPTER VI
The Rules of Engagement for the Formula

The formula is only the essential elements, or ingredients, for getting unstuck. When we are stuck, one or more of the elements for success are missing or are being misapplied. The process for identifying the missing or misapplied elements involves seeking pertinent information by asking a few questions *under the rules of engagement.*

We can compare this process to a game. You wouldn't become consistently successful playing football without first understanding the rules of the game. Becoming skilled in any game would be difficult, at best, without a full understanding of the rules. Likewise, the process of getting unstuck requires that we follow five rules of engagement. We must (1) seek new information, when needed; (2) gain clarity; (3) stay in our own business; (4) practice the actions necessary for success; and (5) anticipate working through moments of chaos that arise before new order is established.

1. Seek new information

In anything new we do, there is a learning curve. A new author must not only write the content for a book, but must also learn about editing, publishing, marketing, pricing and merchandising. If a salesperson wants to change industries, she must learn the products, pricing and sales cycles specific to that industry. She may also need to learn a whole new industry-specific culture. Selling computer products is different from selling oilfield products. Similarly, selling computer products to the oil and gas industry is different from selling them to the medical industry.

We often find ourselves repeating an unproductive pattern because we lack crucial information. We don't know why our actions are not producing success. Seeking out new information gives us new direction, perspective and possibilities.

Seeking out new information gives us new direction, perspective and possibilities.

When I had children, I wanted to parent differently than my parents. I didn't want to yell at my children, use force against them or inadvertently hurt their self-esteem. I wanted our family to be peaceful, loving, and kind. I wanted to respect my children at every age and to be consistent in my parenting. I also wanted to talk to my children about higher education as a norm, rather than as an aspiration. ("When you go to college," as opposed to "*if* you go to college.")

My ideal did not match the only parenting examples I knew—my parents, whose methods were not what I wanted to repeat. I had to seek information about parenting and to learn what was age appropriate for children at all stages of life. I read books about how to talk to (and listen to) children. I read books about parenting and applied the concepts that matched what I wanted to create. Rather than reinventing the wheel, I gathered information from publications written by people who made life-long commitments to studying and teaching successful parenting (as I defined it).

When the path ahead of you is unclear, seek information. Don't recreate the wheel more than necessary. You can find new information from countless sources today. The information age has given us the ability to learn *via* podcasts, videos on demand and audiobooks, to name just a few. We can also learn new information by meeting and talking with people who have already gained the success we want to achieve.

Regardless of the method(s) you use to gain information that you need, remember to use caution to avoid "filtering out" innovative new possibilities. Before sticky-notes were created, people seemed to be happy with paper and tape or thumbtacks.

2. Gain clarity

In this book, I use the term clarity to mean the state of being coherent—logical and consistent—in how we define every facet of the success we are seeking. It is one of the essential elements for success discussed above. At the same time, when applying this handbook's questions (in Chapter VII) that are designed to identify the missing or misapplied elements of success, we need to gain clarity at every step.

A person may *say* that he wants to be a highly-paid professional, such as a doctor or lawyer, but also say he wants to work only 9 a.m. to 5 p.m. on weekdays. He lacks clarity because most highly-paid doctors and lawyers work longer hours and also sometimes respond to calls at night and on weekends. A person may also say that she wants to be a professional, but be unwilling to spend years gaining the required degree(s) and certification(s).

To achieve the parenting style that I defined, I had to find clarity about what I wanted to do differently, and how (methods) to achieve it.

3. Identify (and stay in) your own business

Unless we stay in our own business, we experience the frustration of wanting, but not getting, the change or outcome we desire. People tend to struggle frequently and mightily with this rule of engagement. Generally, when we focus on how others act (or feel) we are not in our business, and things don't change easily. We suffer mentally and emotionally when, instead of focusing on ourselves and our own choices and actions, we want others to change, or we want a different reality. That is why this rule of engagement is often difficult to *master*. Upon mastering it, we give ourselves the best opportunity for the success we are seeking.

When we break this concept down, we have three categories—my business, someone else's business, and reality (things the individual cannot change, which I often call "God's business"). I was first exposed to the concept of the "three businesses" when I read a blog post written by Byron Katie called *Whose Business Are You In?*

My business includes only the things that I can change or affect. Only I can change my intentions, thoughts, beliefs, opinions, words, actions, perspectives and feelings.

Only others can change *their* intentions, thoughts, beliefs, opinions, words, actions, perspectives and feelings. That's their business. And, wow, do we tend to struggle by wanting *them* to change!

"Reality" includes situations and circumstances that are not in any one person's control, such as gravity, weather, disease, disasters, accidents, things that have already happened, etc. Reality is the set of conditions and circumstances in which one is acting or dealing.

Whenever you want to change others or the reality in which you are dealing, you are wasting energy. Focusing on what is in your own control, on the other hand, is very powerful, *solution-oriented energy*. Solution-oriented people don't ignore difficulties or disregard limitations; they choose how to focus their thoughts, words and actions to create progress and well-being.

Being self-focused is different from being self-centered. Self-centeredness is focusing on one's own needs *to the exclusion of* others' needs. Self-focus, on the other hand, is seeking to change only yourself and being the best version of yourself. When we are focused on others' business, we are less logical, productive, efficient and effective. To be most effective, we must focus on what is in our power and control. Self-focus gives you the ability to claim what you want—a successful outcome, as you define it—and continue the course of actions designed to create that result.

It is also important to be the "best version of you." Remember that we can be conscious of our own words and actions. When we speak or act disrespectfully toward another person, or with the intention of causing distress or harm, then we are not being the best we can be. Instead, we are trying to *provoke* the other person. Being the best version of ourselves requires us to speak and act in our most calm, thoughtful, respectful and professional manner.

Conversely, when someone provokes us, such as by using anger, harsh words or actions, we are still in charge of how we respond. If we *react*—meaning a response that is charged with the emotions arising as we hear and experience another person's words or actions—then we only escalate the anger and provocation. If we instead *respond professionally*—calmly and logically—then we are being the best version of ourselves.

When our intentions, communications and actions toward others are thoughtful, respectful and professional, then we are being our best selves and giving others the best opportunity to act in kind. It doesn't guarantee a good response, of course; others always control their own responses to us.

"Be the change you want to see in the world."

–Mahatma Gandhi

My parenting style choices and actions can be used as an example of how to segregate "my business" from "others' business" and "reality." It was my business to decide how to parent my children. It was my business to learn about (and understand) how to teach and guide my children through all of the stages of their growth and development to maturity. The way I showed up to address their behavior (calm and rational, rather than angry and yelling) and the actions I took to guide them were all in *my* business.

Nevertheless, I could not control how my children would feel, respond or react to my parenting. That was in their control—their business. Their reactions might have consequences, but I didn't control their reactions. Sometimes, when our sons were driving us crazy just by doing things typical of children their age, my spouse and I would throw some humor into the situation by saying, "Wow, you're really good at acting age-appropriate." Or, "you're really good at being a teenager!" The funny moment helped us to avoid *reacting* to them in an emotional way and to instead take a minute to choose how to *respond thoughtfully* and *respectfully* to them.

The reality in which I dealt was that my parents did not provide a parenting example I wanted to follow. In my reality, I also had two different children with two different ways of learning, perceiving and responding to the world. Each of them was wired differently at the DNA level. Although they both grew up in our home, each of them also had different life experiences. That reality sometimes required me to adjust the ways I taught each of them.

Turning to a business example, let's consider a project manager for a company that produces a software product. The manager is responsible for the programming of a module (such as the inventory module) of the company's accounting software. The manager has a team of employees who do the programming and report to her. She has certain company assets to help train her programmers in the means and methods in which the company operates and creates its product. She also has the company's employee handbook, which includes company policies such as the dress code, anti-discrimination policy, anti-harassment policy, disciplinary action policy, etc.

In this example, one of the employees assigned to the manager has a habit of reporting late to work in violation of the company policies. It is the manager's business to remind the employee of the hours he is to report to work and to warn the employee of the possibility of being discharged if he cannot consistently report to work on time. The means of communicating with the employee—in compliance with company policies and preferably thoughtfully, respectfully and professionally—is in the manager's business.

It may be in the manager's business to report the employee to human resources whenever he is late to work. If the employee continues to be late after a warning(s), it may be in the manager's business to fire the employee, depending on the manager's level of responsibility and the company's policies.

How the employee responds—whether emotionally or not, respectfully or not, or with action geared to keeping his job (showing up on time) or not—are all in the employee's business. Whether the employee habitually oversleeps is not the manager's business; it's the employee's business. Whether the employee tends to party late on Thursday nights and show up late on Fridays is also the employee's business. The employee's habits, unless changed to conform to the company's expectations, may result in the employee getting fired. But, only the employee controls that.

The employee can *invite* the manager into his business. Alternatively, the manager can offer to talk about anything the employee believes might help with the tardiness issue, hoping to receive an invitation from the employee to discuss any personal problems that may be causing him to be late. But, it's not the manager's business to barge into the employee's personal business unless invited. Uninvited interference with another person's business is rarely, if ever, received well. Stay in your own business, focus on you, and be the best version of you.

4. Practice the actions for success

A new skill is only developed through conscious practice. In my classes I call it the dreaded "P" word. To change a way of thinking is a big endeavor and takes a commitment to practicing on purpose, with purpose.

"Obstacles are those frightful things you see when you take your eyes off your goal."

–Henry Ford

Everything you have, and every success that you have achieved, is within your comfort zone. You already know how to achieve what you already have.

On the other hand, everything you desire that you don't yet already have, is just outside your present comfort zone. By overcoming challenges, and the corresponding discomfort that arises with them, humans evolve, grow, learn and develop skill in choice.

Learning how to identify when we are "in our own business" can be a new skill that takes practice. Using the four handbook questions (Chapter VII) to identify which ingredient(s) for success are missing or being misapplied takes practice.

None of us particularly enjoys the discomfort we feel when we haven't yet practiced a new skill enough to achieve mastery. Regardless, when we find ourselves in a situation and simply do what we have always done—our existing habit instead of our new skill—we will generally get the same results.

We do not practice choice when we show up and only repeat what is familiar or habitual. When we learn a new way of thinking, perceiving, communicating or acting, then we can actively choose to do things differently. Using the four questions *under this and the other rules of engagement*, you can identify where you're stuck and identify a better road to success.

When my kids were young, I often told them, "You don't have to like your sports practice or classes, but you will absolutely like the results!" I don't always like to wash clothes or dishes, but I do enjoy the results. Stay the course and practice this handbook's method until it gets easy.

"The great aim of education is not knowledge but action."

–Herbert Spencer

The longer a pattern has been established, the longer it takes (and the more effort that is required) to transform it into something new. Consider a trail through a field. When people stop walking it, Mother Nature simply reclaims it. The time the trail has been used, as well as the number of people who used it, affects how long it takes Mother Nature to reclaim it. When a culture has a long-existing thought pattern, it takes more time and effort to shift it. Prejudice, for example, is an ancient thought pattern, and it is still being transformed.

> ## "The most difficult thing is the decision to act, the rest is merely tenacity."
>
> *–Amelia Earhart*

Practice makes perfect. Be prepared to practice this handbook to mastery.

5. Expect (and work past) chaos before order

In order to choose and embrace success, we must anticipate that we will experience some chaos before a comfortable new order is established. Whether creating a new product (such as a song, book or technological device), expanding a business, pursuing a new career path or changing a negative dynamic in a relationship with another person, some difficulties and challenges (chaos) will occur before everything is running smoothly. In those moments when you face the inevitable chaos, and you are tempted to stop or turn back, it helps to know that the chaos is temporary. By working through and past it, you ultimately can reach your goal.

FEAR: False Evidence Appearing Real

Consider, for example, an owner of a popular restaurant who wants to enlarge the operations to serve (and profit from) more patrons. If the owner chooses to add another location, additional financing will be needed, a new location must be purchased or leased, furnishings and kitchen products must be purchased, minor or major construction will be necessary, and new staff must be hired and trained. Unexpected complexities will arise in each of those tasks, even if the owner has opened new locations before. Regardless, the additional work required of the owner to complete these tasks, *on top of* those routinely performed for the existing restaurant, constitutes chaos before order is reached in the newly expanded operations.

Another familiar example is what happens when we embark upon a new exercise program to improve health and body appearance. The body resists change, and as a result, gets sore or even sick. We may also feel embarrassingly uncoordinated with the new exercise program. The chaos continues until our body and mind adjusts to the new order—when we can comfortably perform the exercises with confidence, and we recognize improvement in our health, muscle tone and fitness.

Humans tend to prefer to avoid chaos. When it arises, remembering what we are doing (and why) is reassuring; it helps us continue taking the chosen actions necessary to create success—the new order.

CHAPTER VII
The Questions

1. **What?**

2. **Why?**

3. **How?**

4. **How will I know I'm successful?**

Before you decide that these four questions are a little too simplistic to figure out why you're stuck, don't be hasty! Admittedly, in every area of your life in which you have already achieved success, you consciously (or unconsciously) applied all four of these questions. In fact, you unconsciously apply them to the simplest daily decisions. When you're stuck, these questions (used under the rules of engagement) will help you identify what is blocking (missing from) the success you seek. My experience, both personal and gained through working with clients, has shown me the complex challenges that can arise when applying these questions under the rules of engagement. Nevertheless, my clients and I have found significant relief and positive rewards from overcoming obstacles in the road to success.

The more you refine—gain clarity (Rule of Engagement #2)—in each of these questions and your answers, the better you can achieve the essential elements for success. If you are wishy-washy about your answers to the questions, you might not achieve the greatest success or attain the best experience possible.

In this introduction, we will explore a day-to-day example of when you have likely *unconsciously* used these questions to create a good experience. Then, as we address each of the four questions in more depth, we will illustrate the process through an example of a person who is stuck when trying to decide a more complicated, career-oriented issue.

Let's explore the process with the day-to-day example of deciding to go to a restaurant for dinner. The "What" applies to your desire, such as delicious food, cooked and served by someone else. You gain clarity in your "What" by being more specific, such as identifying a particular type of food, a particular type of ambience, a price-range, etc. You can gain more clarity by identifying what you want to do while eating, such as watching sports on televisions, having a quiet conversation, or having a lively discussion with friends.

The question "Why" is used to identify the reasons for "What" you desired. You may have been tired and preferred to avoid the extra chores of cooking and cleaning up afterward. Your pantry may have been bare, and you might not have wanted to go to the grocery store. The question "How" also provided more specifics, such as the distance you were willing to drive, whether you would drive with or separately from others, and the time you planned to meet for dinner, etc.

The question "How will I know I'm successful" was used as a benchmark against your desire. If you defined your "What" as enjoying delicious upscale burgers and fries, with an average entrée price of $20 or less, and enjoyed watching many kinds of sports on the restaurant's televisions, then you would have a clear idea during and after the meal as to whether you were successful in selecting the restaurant.

We all use a similar thought process when applied to big events in our lives, such as planning a wedding, planning a vacation, or buying a car, house or business. It's when we get stuck that we can get lost. Sometimes we don't even know where to begin to find out why we're stuck. Although these four straightforward questions seem like a simplistic approach, they can lead to a deep dive into finding our way to personal success. With each step, we can discover where we lack or misapply clarity, belief, action or consistency.

The What: Know your target, your goal, your "end in mind." What do you want? What do you want to achieve or accomplish? Be able to state and write it clearly and concisely. If you are not sure precisely what you want, you may have to begin by listing what you don't want. It's fine to back into the clarity.

Let's use a practical example based on the programming project manager we discussed in the rules of engagement chapter above. In this example, she has been a successful project manager for over five years and feels stuck in her career path. She doesn't know why she hasn't yet been promoted to "senior project manager," which usually occurs within five years of becoming a project manager in the company where she works. She doesn't know whether she wants to continue pursuing the career ladder there, or whether she wants to pursue moving to a consulting company. She has also considered an entrepreneurial venture of her own, programming websites for businesses and individuals.

She doesn't yet know precisely what she wants. She needs to gather more information (Rule of Engagement, or "ROE" #1) to help her concisely identify her desire. Note also that, if her sole desire had been to get promoted to senior manager, then she would be violating ROE #3 (be in our own business) because it is the company's business to decide who it promotes; the company sets its requirements for promotion. Other than improving her performance to match the company's specifications, she has no control over the process of getting promoted.

First, she needs to gain clarity (ROE #2) regarding her preferences and needs. For example, she needs clarity about: (1) the working conditions that she wants in her next career step; (2) the income she is seeking; (3) the hours she wants to work; (4) the location(s) she is willing to work; (5) the amount of travel, if any, she is willing to accept; (6) the means and manner of maintaining her life balance; (7) perquisites, such as bonuses and vacation schedules; and (8) anything else she feels she needs to make her feel successful and fulfilled.

Because she is considering staying with the company where she is currently working, but hasn't yet been promoted to the position of senior manager, she needs to find out what criteria the company requires of its senior managers. (ROE #1). She needs to know which of those criteria she has not yet met. In short, she must talk to her supervisor (and potentially others who are involved in promotion decisions) to get guidance about what the company believes she must do in order to be promoted.

She is also considering changing her career path to go into consulting. She should gather information (ROE #1) about the hours consultants work, the way consultants are compensated (salaried, by the job, hourly, etc.), the amount of travel required, etc. She would want to know whether she could occasionally work from home and whether most of her work would be done at the consulting company's location, as opposed to its client's offices.

Because she is considering starting a web-designing business, she needs to learn more information (ROE #1) about the market, costs of operations, target customers, price points and rates for website design, the competition, etc. She needs to know her marketing plans to drive the right potential customers to her business. She must also gather legal and accounting advice for the formation of, and accounting for, her business.

Let's presume that she has spent time considering the general custom-tailored issues outlined above and has decided:

1. She wants to maximize her earning potential over the long-term, and her minimum pay for the next job is $100,000;

2. She is a mother and wants to be able to attend some of her children's activities, such as sports, dance, etc., so she wants relatively predictable hours, preferably 9 a.m. to 5 p.m. on weekdays, with little or no overtime or weekend work;

3. She is willing to travel, but preferably no more than a total of one week per month;

4. She prefers to have no more than a 30 minute daily commute each direction;

5. She prefers to work for a company with 10 or more employees because she likes the social interaction in her business day; and She wants to have at least 2 weeks of vacation per year, and preferably three.

These decisions can have great impact on the final selection of her desired career path. For example, her entrepreneurial idea may conflict (at least at first) with her minimum pay of $100,000 per year, and her preference to work for a company of 10 or more employees.

Her preference to work only on weekdays from 9 a.m. to 5 p.m. likely conflicts with a consulting job, because consultants are known for working beyond those hours and on weekends. Her preferred hours also likely conflict with her entrepreneurial aspirations until she builds the business sufficiently to hire people and leverage the work.

Her limitation on traveling may also conflict with many consulting positions because consultants sometimes travel to remote job sites on a weekly or monthly basis for months on end.

These and other considerations all help provide her clarity. She is backing into the determination of "What" she wants, and ultimately she may need to decide where she is willing to make compromises in defining her next career step.

The Why: We ask "Why," in part, to gain clarity about our "What." Why do we want our stated desire? Because it helps us ensure that we will zealously pursue our goal. Without clarity on the "Why," we may fail to follow through with our intention.

Building success requires a strong emotional commitment. Emotions are energy in motion; when you can access the emotion behind your "Why," you've engaged personally and powerfully with your desire. Dare to use your energy (your passion) to help propel you toward your desire.

Lack of clarity creates less than clear results— in anything here on earth.

Asking "Why" we want something also ensures that our desire is authentic—something we want, rather than what someone else wants or what someone else may want for us. Throughout this book, I have been referring to finding success, "however you define it." Success is more easily obtained and enjoyed when it is uniquely yours—fits your deeply true and personal preferences, wishes and ambitions.

**"Your beliefs become your thoughts,
Your thoughts become your words,
Your words become your actions,
Your actions become your habits,
Your habits become your values,
Your values become your destiny."**

–Mahatma Gandhi

It is not unusual, however, when answering the question "Why" that you might find you have been repeating someone else's wishes—those of your friends, parents or other loved ones—instead of your own. Alternatively, you might not have updated your wishes. As we gain more experience in life, our desires sometimes change. Our definitions of success may also change.

As an example, let's turn back to our project manager and the three career paths she is considering. She has interest in seeking further promotion in her current job because she is comfortable with the company and can continue to gain personal and professional growth there. She likes the company's culture and work environment. The work that the company's senior project managers perform is a good fit for her and would look good on her resumé. She could also continue to have dependable hours and the ability to balance her personal and professional lives.

Consulting, on the other hand, could provide significantly more income and more exciting challenges. It would also likely require her to work far more demanding hours. She believes the expanded work hours, weekend work and travel might be a better fit in her life balance when her children are older.

Our project manager is interested in an entrepreneurial pursuit—a website building business—because she believes she will enjoy more control, flexibility and financial growth that can arise from building her own business. She has built high-quality, functional websites for friends and family without charge, and she enjoyed the work. She imagines having more control over her career because she would not be laid off in a downturn. At worst, she believes that a downturn might cause her revenues to decline (and might cause her to have need to lay off some/all staff she might one day have); however, she would still have the business income that she could generate. She imagines being able to occasionally work from home. She anticipates having more flexibility in timing her own travel or vacations. At the same time, she realizes that many new businesses fail in the first three years. She knows that she would have to build clientele and a growing income stream, which means making do without the six-figure income she prefers.

Our project manager may need to spend significant time with her choices, allowing herself to feel where her underlying needs and desires are strongest. She will need to find clarity (ROE #2) with the direction that fits *all four* of the handbook questions—What, Why, How and How Will I Know I'm Successful. She might get deeply into the "How" or "How Will I Know I'm Successful" questions, and then realize she must go back and redefine her "What" and/or her "Why." The "Why" is as personal, and as important, as the "What."

Spend time with your "Why." Dig in deep to find your unique, authentic "What."

The How: The question "How" asks for the entire plan of action for creating or achieving the "What"—a concrete written list. The plan definitely includes identifying and listing issues that need research (ROE #1), confirming we are in our own business (ROE #3) and gaining clarity on all of the steps necessary to reach the goal (ROE #2). It involves setting goals and creating checklists of all the steps necessary to achieve the goal. The question "How" also helps formulate accountability for the process of achieving your goal, just as project meetings help ensure a business that a new project is proceeding on schedule and in budget. The "How" is the layout of all of the actions that will need to be done, and consistently practiced (ROE #4), through and beyond any chaos that arises before the goal is attained (ROE #5). Furthermore, finding clarity when asking "How" includes being strategic when looking at both the present and the future.

The "How" is about getting your thoughts, emotions and energy engaged with what you want by strategizing all of the action steps involved.

For our project manager, who has not yet decided which potential path to pursue (her "What"), she must identify the "How" for each path she is considering.

For our example, let's presume that our project manager has decided, for the time being, to pursue a promotion to senior project manager with her existing employer. This will require, among other things: (1) meeting with her supervisor to learn what requirements and targets must be achieved to be considered for the promotion; (2) identifying what written company requirements exist for the senior project manager job description so she can be certain she meets them; (3) conferring with other senior project managers about how they overcame any challenges to attaining the position; (4) conferring with senior project managers about their day-to-day work and the challenges they routinely face so that she will be best prepared for them; (5) working with her supervisor and any other persons in management to formulate and approve an action plan to help her achieve the position.

In addition, our project manager will want to ensure that she is gaining skills that will help her both now and in her *future* career paths, including the path of consulting, which she thinks might be a better fit when her children are older. She may want to be proactive by gaining information about the programming languages and project management skills that are most marketable in consulting companies. To the extent she has the ability, she might seek project management assignments that will give her the strongest resumé for being hired in the future by a consulting company.

Most businesspersons are familiar with the concept of Smart Goals, which require tangible and measurable actions that lead to the results you seek. When answering "How," these types of goals are very helpful.

SMART GOALS

S — Specific, strategic, self-reliable, sincere, simple, straight-forward.

M — Measurable, motivating, manageable, mapped to the result.

A — Achievable, agreed, adaptable, ambitious, accountable, attainable.

R — Realistic, reliable, result-oriented, recordable.

T — Time bounded, time relatable, trackable, tangible, team building.

Some versions also ad ER to form SmartER goals

E — Encompassing, evaluable, engaged, exciting.

R — Reviewed, realistic, realizable.

Smart Goals are equally helpful when people are seeking a type of success that is more conceptual or less tangible. People sometimes tell me they want to be happy, but they don't think about "How" to gain happiness in a strategic, focused, measurable way. They may not know where to begin to make a checklist or "to do" list to create the happiness they seek. They may need to seek new information (ROE #1) about the science of human happiness. There are many books on happiness that I can recommend. *The Charge* by Brendon Burchard describes 10 human drives that are essential for happiness. *Happy for No Reason* by Marci Shimoff describes practices geared to increase one's capacity to experience more happiness. *The Science of Happiness* is a another book and is offered as a MOOC (Massive Open Online Courses) designed for learning science-based principles and practices for attaining a happy life.

Once a person identifies her goal for happiness and learns more about methods to achieve it, she still needs to create and apply Smart Goals to guarantee follow-through all the way to success.

If you want the most positive personal experience when working through the process of achieving your goal, be true to the rules of engagement. Otherwise, you can have the best heartfelt intentions and still inadvertently create unwanted drama.

> **We want the energy of our heart
> to be free to create well.
> To do that, we need our minds to
> follow the rules of engagement.**

Our heart energy can be strong and well-intended, but if we don't use our minds to apply the rules of engagement, the results can be disappointing or even traumatizing. A nurse, for example, may hear a patient complaining about her family or other life circumstances unrelated to the patient's physical condition. If the nurse steps into the role of friend, counselor or amateur psychologist and offers uninvited advice, even with the best intentions, the patient is likely to become furious. The nurse's intentions were heart-centered, but the rules of engagement were not applied; she was outside of her own business (ROG #3), and she did not ask the patient whether she was open to hearing any personal advice.

How will you know you're successful?

This step is often overlooked and misinterpreted because it involves not only listing tangible benchmarks for gauging whether you are achieving the milestones toward your ultimate success, but it also requires you to define *how you will feel* when you are successful.

Most people are accustomed to setting benchmarks to assess their status toward reaching a goal. A salesperson wanting to reach a high level of success would anticipate a certain number of sales calls and sales per month, with growing sales over time.

Quantitative benchmarks are very helpful, but benchmarks that assess our personal satisfaction are even more powerful. People want something because they believe (consciously or unconsciously) that it will make them feel a particular way. If they don't feel the way they believed they would, then they can be disillusioned with the success.

Let's return to our software project manager example. If she says she will know she is successful when she gets the promotion she is pursuing, she is choosing a benchmark for success that is outside of her business and control (ROE #2). She can do everything within her power to satisfy the company's prerequisites to be considered for promotion, but only the company can promote her. She will have competition for the position, and others' performance might outshine hers.

Her benchmark also fails to describe how she will *feel* successful. We don't know from her stated benchmark whether she is seeking personal validation, professional growth, happiness, etc.

Examples of more effective ways for our project manager to define "How She Will Know She's Successful" include:

- I will show up each day happy about, and grateful for, my ability to continue working in a company with a great corporate culture and work environment.

- I will show up for work each day feeling enthused about being the best project manager I know how to be.

- I will feel that I made a powerful choice to continue reaching for the senior project manager job.

- I will enjoy the process of learning how the company evaluates and selects its senior project managers.

- I will feel good about committing a specified number of months/years to pursue the promotion.

- I will feel good about gaining additional experience that will strengthen my resumé for advancement, both within the company, as well as potentially with a consulting firm someday.

- I will have gratitude for my continued work/personal life balance, which I value immensely.

- I will relish enjoying my children's activities without significant work-related travel.

- All of these benchmarks are within her business and control. None of them depend on the company's, or anyone else's, actions.

Often, when people create their "How Will I Know I'm Successful" lists, they realize for the first time that they are reaching for things that are either: (1) outside of their business; or (2) sought for the benefit of persons other than themselves (pleasing a spouse, parent, boss, etc.). When this happens, they must go back and redefine (clarify) their "What."

When I prepared my parenting plan, I knew that many things outside of my control could happen—accidents, brain injuries, disease, addiction and innumerable other undesirable things. Regardless of anything my children might experience, or how they might feel, I knew that I would be consistent in intelligently responding to my children through their ever-changing developmental stages, without emotionally charged reactions.

Recap of the Handbook Questions

These four handbook questions, used under the rules of engagement, help you continuously feed your desires. In the process, you will find which of the essential elements of success you have been missing or misapplying in the past: clarity, belief, action and/or consistency.

As illustrated through our applications of these four questions, you can discover that you either lacked (or misapplied) one or more of the four essential elements for the success (your "What") that you have been seeking. You may have lacked clarity in any of the four areas—"What" you want to achieve, "Why" you want it, "How" you get it, or "How You Will Know You Were Successful." You could have dropped one or more of the rules of engagement—staying in your own business (ROE #3) being the one most often violated.

You might have lacked the necessary belief. Belief is achieved when thought and feeling are strongly intertwined. If you weren't sufficiently emotionally engaged in your target, then you would lack essential belief. If, for example, you chose a target to please someone else (or because someone else thought it would be good for you), your own belief system may not have fully bought into the target.

In the process of going through these questions, and assessing your progress against your benchmarks, you may have found a lack of consistency. We can't just brush our teeth once per month and expect to have great dental hygiene. We can't just exercise once per week and expect to be physically fit. We can't be a successful businessperson without keeping regular work hours. We have to logically and consistently stretch for, and work at achieving, our goals on a daily, weekly and monthly basis.

You may not enjoy
the consistent practice,
but you will enjoy
the results.

CHAPTER VIII
Judgment Versus Preference

We live in a culture that is often about blaming others. This is energy spent with zero return on investment ("ROI"). We are hard-programmed to be right (survival instinct), so our minds are continually working to identify and label what is right and what is wrong, especially about others and their ideas and concepts.

Whenever we are in judgment of someone or something, we are creating a judge and victim, and we are limiting our ability to overcome challenges. For example, a person working for a business may be frustrated when the company updates its computer systems and software. For many people, learning a new system is highly uncomfortable. When the person thinks, "We shouldn't change things up just when we all know how to work this system," she is in judgment—judging the company for its decisions, judging the software (easy or not), judging the time-consuming learning curve (quick or slow). She is only adding pain to the process she must go through to keep working for the company. What we resist persists. Instead, choose solution-oriented thought.

Let's consider an example in which judgment can limit a person's opportunities. If a businessperson is interested in pursuing a goal, but believes his spouse will not support it, he is in judgment—a more subtle right and wrong. In essence, he is judging (and blaming her) for bypassing an opportunity without first giving it a chance. If, instead, he takes time to clearly identify his "What," "Why," "How," and "How Will I Know I Am Successful," then he may list benefits not only for himself, but also for his spouse and family that his spouse has never considered. Having found that clarity, he may then sit down with his spouse and discuss the possibilities. She might identify additional benefits that he had not yet considered. Together, they could explore concessions that can allow him to pursue his new goal *with her support.* By giving something a chance without pre-judging how it will be received by others, you might be pleasantly surprised by the positive reception you get when you show up with the four essential elements for success.

Similar examples can be easily imagined in the corporate context. "Oh, the boss will never go for that!" "The company has always done things that way; they'll never consider my idea." Focusing instead on what you prefer, rather than on a concept of "right and wrong," allows you to be more creative and self-empowered.

Here's one last tip about judgment. Whenever you say any kind of 'woulda, coulda, shoulda' statement, you're in judgment and out of your business. If you're talking about what someone else could or should have done, that's their business. If you're wishing you had done something better in the past, then you're actually in the business of reality. Most of us would do many things differently in the past if we only had today's knowledge and experience. Be thoughtful, respectful and professional in dealings with everyone, including yourself.

Remember: Judgment contracts and separates. Preference, on the other hand, accepts and expands our possibilities.

CHAPTER IX
Examples - Applying the Handbook Questions

Example 1: Imagine a woman who has decided to contact her birth father who she had met a time or two many years ago and who had not been involved in her life otherwise. She plans to reach out to see if he wants to know his grandchildren. She did, but found herself stuck in anger and resentment, because her birth father and his spouse thought she was really out to get money from them.

Let's analyze her application of the handbook questions to her objective:

1. Her **What**: Reach out to her birth father.

2. Her **Why**: She wanted to know inner peace in that she offered the possibility of a relationship between him and his grandchildren.

3. Her **How**: Find his number and call.

4. Her **How She Knew She Was Successful**: None.

By leaving out the fourth question, she found herself drawn into judgment and her birth father's irrational emotional reactions. Unconsciously, she had created an expectation of a different (much more positive response or outcome) from her father. Only her father is responsible for his reaction (ROE #3).

If, however, she had defined her answer to the fourth question as: I intend to contact him, offer the relationship and leave the decision-making (including any reactions) up to him, then she would have felt successful without being disappointed in his decision and reactions.

Example 2: Consider a man who is struggling to help his mother, who lives in a distant state and whose health is fragile. The man's work commitments limit his ability to travel to his mother. Without continuing to be successful with his job, he won't have sufficient funds to help his mother in her senior years.

His answers to the handbook questions are:

1. His **What**: Make his mother happy.

2. His **Why**: He loves his mother and wants to be a good son. He also wants her to be safe and have access to good healthcare.

3. His **How**: Many phone calls, organizing a place for her to live, as well as health care professionals to assess and treat her, as needed. Arranging regular payment for his mother's living expenses and care.

4. His **How He Knew He Was Successful**: His mother would be happy.

The problems here are clear. His mother's happiness is her business, not his. We can never guarantee another's happiness, no matter what we provide.

A better "What" would not depend on his mother's happiness. He could focus on providing for her needs in light of his best understanding of her preferences. He could, for example, find living situations in her home state, rather than his own, because she prefers staying near her friends. He could focus on being the best son that he could be, under his own definition. He could, for example, make many phone calls to relatives and service providers, sorting out logistics and payment, and using patience with his mother in the process. (His "How.") His benchmark for "How He Would Know He Was Successful" could be delivering everything he can, within his means, with respect, patience and thoughtfulness.

Example 3: Let's consider a woman suffering with social anxiety. Whether a person is prescribed medication to help with the anxiety, it often doesn't resolve the anxiety completely. If the woman must go to a party with friends and co-workers, these might be her handbook questions:

1. Her **What**: Have the best possible time she can at a work social event.

2. Her **Why**: To be comfortable, socially. She wants to show up and interact with coworkers for the business aspect.

3. Her **How**: Dressing comfortably and showing up on time. Being the best listener and circulating to say "hello." Ask good questions to start conversations with key people. Have a time to leave and firm reason why she will leave at that time.

4. Her **How Will I Know I'm Successful**: She will feel good about going, and will feel good about how she interacted with everyone.

You'll notice that her focus was not about her feeling like a social butterfly; instead, she focused on defining her success in terms of how she showed up for, and communicated throughout, the event.

Example 4: A man is preparing for job interviews.

1. His **What**: Have successful (by his standards) interviews.

2. His **Why**: To maximize the possibilities of receiving job offers.

3. His **How**: Doing his research on the company, its products and services, and the positions for which they are hiring. Being prepared to ask good questions that will let him know whether the company and job is a good fit. Staying mentally present and answering questions honestly. Being comfortable and interested in the interviewer. Trusting himself to listen and respond appropriately.

4. His **How Will I Know I'm Successful**: Feeling confident I did my best by being conscious and responding. Knowing I have no control over being hired, only over how I showed up in interview.

Many people mistakenly think it's only a good interview if they are hired. The hiring decision is totally out of their business; it's solely in the company's control. There are many moving parts that the interviewee can neither know nor predict. Whether or not a person is hired is a business decision based on numbers, the company's needs and timing.

Example 5: A woman wants to support a friend who is grieving:

1. Her **What**: Being supportive with a grieving friend.

2. Her **Why**: She cares for her friend and wants to be a good friend in an uncomfortable situation.

3. Her **How**: Learn about grief. Avoid rushing or offering advice. Avoiding saying clichés out of discomfort and lack of experience with others who are grieving.

4. Her **How Will I Know I'm Successful**: Listen with her heart without offering advice or clichés. Be patient and non-judgmental. Listen as if it is her sole job and contribution. Follow the grieving friend's lead, and respond appropriately. Feel good staying the course of the compassionate listener.

Example 6: An adult student is struggling with a teacher he has paid for a 12 week course. He has argued with the teacher and pointed out how he would prefer that the class be taught. He has unintentionally caused resistance, conflict and annoyance to himself, the teacher and the other students.

He didn't do the handbook questions and was unhappy with the class. His stated goal was to get the skill or certification that came from the class. But, he had not realized he was acting as though his "What" was to receive a different style of teaching.

He might have had a better experience if his handbook questions were:

1. His **What**: Getting the skill or certification.

2. His **Why**: He is interested in learning the skills being taught.

3. His **How**: By listening, studying, following directions. Showing up prepared, rested and ready for tests. Being respectful of the teacher, the teacher's style (even if not what he preferred) and the other students.

4. His **How Will I Know I'm Successful**: Completion of the course without drama or trauma!

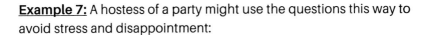

Example 7: A hostess of a party might use the questions this way to avoid stress and disappointment:

1. Her **What**: Create and enjoy her party.

2. Her **Why**: To celebrate and connect.

3. Her **How**: Planning in advance. Making lists. Delegating (flowers, food, photos, cleanup, etc.). Being rested and dressed on time. Greeting each guest with warmth, gratitude and a personalized, appropriate question of what is new in their life.

4. Her **How Will I Know I'm Successful**: I will feel relaxed and connected to everyone. I will enjoy laughter, food and people.

Example 8: For this book, my handbook questions were:

1. My **What**: An easy to read book on the short version of principle based thought that allows me to reach more people.

2. My **Why**: To follow through with Karen and open doors to contributing in new arenas.

3. My **How**:
   - Sit and write until the inspiration flows.
   - Read and edit, and read out loud to see if makes sense and flows.
   - Get feedback from a few people.
   - Pay an editor.
   - Pay for cover and layout.
   - Pay for printing and order books.
   - Set up on Amazon.

4. My **How I'll Know I'm Successful**: I'll be getting feedback through sales and testimonies. I'll contribute information to more people than I am now. I'll feel like I did my best on the book and feel confident in sharing and selling it.

You'll notice that my success doesn't depend on numbers I'd naturally hope for. What others do is out of my personal control so it is not my business. The sales and testimonies aren't my business either, although I naturally hope that it may follow. My intention is different from that of someone who has already written books and has an established audience for their written work. We must always define success appropriately based on our unique circumstances.

I really don't know what surprises life will bring next. I do, however, know how I'll show up because I know how to think, which allows me to have the best experience of me.

I hope these examples have given you a glimpse of how powerful these simple questions and the rules of engagement can be in identifying where you're stuck and propelling you into the success you seek. I hope they have created a better understanding of what is possible when you choose clarity, belief, action and consistency on purpose, with purpose.

THIS IS MY WISH FOR YOU:

Courage to consistently live up to your potential;
Faith to hold steady on your journey into
your unique success;
Ease and **Humor** along the way;
Power in knowing of your authentic desires;
Success, **Health** and **Happiness** for you and yours!

THIS IS MY COMMITMENT TO YOU:

Authentically supporting and guiding those seeking to
thrive into the best experience of themselves in the most
direct, efficient route by providing Transformative Vibration,
Knowledge and Presence.

Helen Racz